before
amen

before amen

THE POWER OF A SIMPLE PRAYER

NEW YORK TIMES BEST-SELLING AUTHOR

MAX LUCADO

WRITTEN BY KEVIN AND SHERRY HARNEY

THOMAS NELSON
Since 1798

NASHVILLE   MEXICO CITY   RIO DE JANEIRO

Published in Nashville, Tennessee, by Thomas Nelson. Thomas Nelson is a registered trademark of Thomas Nelson, Inc.

Published in association with Anvil II Management, Inc.

Thomas Nelson, Inc. titles may be purchased in bulk for educational, business, fund-raising, or sales promotional use. For information, please e-mail SpecialMarkets@ThomasNelson.com.

All Scripture quotations, unless otherwise indicated, are taken from The Holy Bible, *New International Version®, NIV®*. Copyright © 1973, 1978, 1984, 2011 by Biblica, Inc.™ Used by permission. All rights reserved worldwide.

Scripture quotations marked NKJV are taken from the New King James Version. Copyright © 1982 by Thomas Nelson, Inc. Used by permission. All rights reserved.

Scripture quotations marked NLT are taken from the *Holy Bible, New Living Translation*, copyright © 1996, 2004. Used by permission of Tyndale House Publishers, Inc., Wheaton, Illinois. All rights reserved.

Any Internet addresses (websites, blogs, etc.) and telephone numbers in this book are offered as a resource. They are not intended in any way to be or imply an endorsement by Thomas Nelson, nor does Thomas Nelson vouch for the content of these sites and numbers for the life of this book.

Cover design and photography: Micah Kandros
Interior design: Matthew Van Zomeren

ISBN: 978-0-5291-2334-3

First Printing August 2014 / Printed in the United States of America

14 15 16 17 18 RRD 6 5 4 3 2 1

Contents

Of Note

The quotations interspersed throughout this study guide and the introductory comments are excerpts from the book *Before Amen* and the video curriculum of the same name by Max Lucado. All other resources—including the small group questions, session introductions, and between-sessions materials—have been written by Kevin and Sherry Harney.

A Word from Max Lucado

Do you want to learn to pray? I would suggest that there is no better place to start than watching Jesus as he prayed — and watching him very closely.

Jesus set a compelling prayer example. He prayed before he ate. He prayed for children. He prayed for the sick. He prayed for the downtrodden. He made the planets and shaped the stars, yet he prayed. He is the Lord of angels and commander of heavenly hosts, yet he prayed. He was coequal with God, the exact representation of the Holy One, yet he devoted himself to prayer. He prayed in the desert, in the cemetery, and in the garden. "He went out and departed to a solitary place; and there He prayed" (Mark 1:35 NKJV).

This dialog must have been common among his friends.

"Has anyone seen Jesus?"

"Oh, you know. He's up to the same thing."

"Praying, *again*?"

"Yep. He's been gone since sunrise."

Jesus was prone to disappear for an entire night of prayer. I'm thinking of one occasion in particular. He had just experienced one of the most stressful days of his ministry. The morning began with the news of the brutal execution of his cousin, John the Baptist. Jesus sought to retreat with his disciples, yet a throng of thousands followed him. Though he was grief-stricken, he spent the day teaching and healing people. When the disciples discovered that the host of people had no food to eat, Jesus multiplied bread out of a basket and fed the entire multitude. In the span of twelve hours, he battled sorrow, stress, demands, and needs. He deserved a good night's rest. Yet, when evening finally came, he told the crowd to leave and the disciples to board their boat, and "he went up into the hills by himself to pray" (Mark 6:46 NLT).

Apparently, it was the correct choice. A storm exploded over the Sea of Galilee, leaving the disciples "in trouble far away from land, for a strong wind had risen, and they were fighting heavy waves. About three o'clock in the morning Jesus came toward them, walking on the water" (Matthew 14:24–25 NLT). Jesus ascended the mountain depleted. He reappeared invigorated. When he reached the water, he never broke his stride. You'd have thought the water was a park lawn and the storm a spring breeze.

Do you think the disciples made the prayer/power connection? "Lord, teach us to pray *like that*." Teach us to find strength in prayer. To banish fear in prayer. To defy storms in prayer. To come off the mountain of prayer with the authority of a prince.

What about you? The disciples faced angry waves and a watery grave. You face angry clients, a turbulent economy, stormy family challenges, and the raging seas of stress and sorrow. If you are like the disciples, you might find yourself asking Jesus, "Will you teach me to pray?" If you want to learn, there is no better teacher than Jesus. If you are ready, there is no better time than now.

I am delighted that we are taking this prayer journey together!

Father, You Are Good

How should we draw near to God? Come like a little child. That was the advice of Jesus. Come carefree. Joy-filled. Playful. Trusting. Curious. Excited. Forget greatness; seek littleness. Trust more, strut less. Make lots of requests and accept all the gifts. Come to God like a child comes to Daddy.

Introduction

Insane complexity.

It is everywhere, seeking to swallow us up. It shouts so loud we can barely hear ourselves think. In many cases, it makes no sense. But the countless options, endless flavors, and infinite opportunities slam against our lives like a tsunami.

If you are more than fifty years old, you probably remember a time when there were only three TV channels. There was a time at night when a voice came on the television to say, "This concludes today's programing." After that announcement, the TV went blank! There was nothing to watch.

If you are under thirty, you can't imagine a world without hundreds of channels available twenty-four hours a day providing cooking shows, shopping networks, sports, movies, situation comedies, children's programming, "reality" shows, religious shows, news, and programs about virtually anything you can imagine. You can sit down to relax and watch a half hour of TV and spend the entire time wading through the sea of options, never settling on something entertaining or relaxing.

Suppose you wanted to learn about fly-fishing. Years ago, you would find someone who loved the sport and have a conversation with him or her. You might check out a book about fly-fishing from the local library. If you were really motivated, you could go out and watch an actual person artistically dance a fly across the waters of a stream. But today, if you want to get an introduction to fly-fishing, all you have to do is a Google search. Within a fraction of a second, you will have at your disposal more than ninety million online articles, videos, sales promotions, pictures, and perspectives on this one topic.

Into our complex world, Jesus calls us to prayer. His invitation is gentle and quite simple. Be honest. Be yourself. There are not a lot of rules. You don't need ninety million articles and videos to learn to pray. Just talk with your heavenly Father and be confident that he hears you, he loves you, and he is good.

> Prayer is simply a heartfelt conversation between God and his child.

Talk About It

What are some of the things we do that make prayer more complex than it needs to be?

or

Who taught you to pray? What did he or she teach you?

Video Teaching Notes

As you watch the video teaching segment for Session 1 featuring Max Lucado, use the following outline to record anything that stands out to you.

A member of the PGA (Prayer Giants Association) or the PWA (Prayer Wimps Association)

Why we pray

The disciples' sign-up sheet for Prayer 101 with Jesus

A simple, easy-to-remember, pocket-sized prayer: *Father, you are good. I need help. They need help. Thank you. In Jesus' name, amen.*

The launch pad of prayer: "Oh, Daddy"

How to pray and how not to pray

Prayer expresses trust and also builds trust

Before you face the world, face your Father.

Video Discussion and Bible Study

1. Talk about your personal experience with prayer. Be honest
   as to whether you struggle or excel. Just share your journey.

2. Tell about a person in your life who models passionate and
   natural prayer. What drives that person to pray? What have
   you learned by observing his or her intimate communica-
   tion with God?

3. Max says, "We all have our doubts about prayer." Describe a time when you struggled with prayer. What questions did you ask? How honest were you with God? How has God taken you a few steps forward as a person of prayer through your doubting process?

Prayer is the hand of faith on the door handle of your heart.

Read: Matthew 6:9–13

4. What are some of the key topics Jesus teaches his followers to focus on in this prayer? Why are these topics simple yet very important?

Max offers a little prayer—a springboard—to launch us into conversation with God on some of the epic and massive yet simple topics of life. Here is the prayer:

Father, you are good.
I need help.
They need help.
Thank you.
In Jesus' name, amen.

> ## Let the pocket-sized prayer punctuate your day.

5. Max says that "Oh, Daddy" is a good way to begin a prayer. What are some of the various ways we can address God? What does each attribute, quality, or name mean as we speak to God in prayer?

> ## God's unrivaled goodness undergirds everything else we can say about prayer.

6. If we truly approached God as a dear, loved, tender Daddy, what kind of interaction would mark our conversation with him?

Read: Matthew 6:5–8

7. How have you seen prayer become a production or an opportunity for spiritual showing off? How have you seen this kind of attitude and practice find its way into your own conversations with God, either in private or in public?

God is low on fancy, high on accessibility.

Read: Isaiah 46:9 and Genesis 1:1–5, 26–27

8. Why can you trust God when it comes to your life and prayers? What has God done in your life to show you that he is trustworthy? What is one action you can take that will show God and the people around you that you know he is good and trustworthy?

9. In the video presentation, Max gives a snapshot of how one person might start the day in prayer. Of course, it will look different for each person. What might a day of prayer look like in your life if you took the lesson of today's study seriously? In particular, what specific and practical thing could you do during *one* of these times of the day to show God that you trust him and know he is good?

❑ When you first wake up, before you get out of bed …

❑ As you encounter family members or roommates where you live …

❑ As you work, go to school, or engage in your vocation …

❑ When you face a point of tension or conflict …

❑ When something good and joy-filled happens …

If God were only mighty, we would salute him. But since he is merciful and mighty, we can approach him.

Closing Prayer

Take time as a group to pray in any of the following directions:

- Thank God for someone in your life who has been a consistent example of simple, authentic, passionate prayer.
- Confess where you have been a prayer wimp and let God know that you want to learn to pray with greater passion and authenticity.
- Tell God some of the ways you have experienced his goodness.
- Thank God for being a loving and present Father.
- Thank God for hanging in there with you, even when you struggled with doubts and questions.

Just as a happy child cannot mis-hug,
the sincere heart cannot mis-pray.

Between Sessions

Personal Reflection

Take time in personal reflection to think about the following questions:

- What are some of the ways I pray that are natural and flow out of a simple understanding of God as my Father—as my Daddy? How can I develop this part of my prayer life?

- What are some bad habits, routines, or attitudes that have seeped into my life of prayer? What can I do to minimize and remove these?

- What experiences have caused me to question God's goodness and wonder if he really cares about me or hears my prayers? How can I talk with God about these specific things that keep me from praying with confidence?

- How do I tend to address God in prayer? How has God been like a loving Father to me? How could I address him with more intimate and trusting names?

- Are there certain times or situations when my prayers tend to become more of a production? How can I seek greater authenticity in these moments?

Personal Actions

Starting Your Day with a Pocket-Sized Prayer

For the next week, start each day lifting up this simple prayer. Commit it to memory (this should take only a few minutes).

Father,
You are good.
I need help.
They need help.
Thank you.
In Jesus' name, amen.

Say this prayer out loud. Emphasize one line at a time, and then build on that line. When you pray, "I need help," linger there and talk with your Father about a few areas of your life where you really *do* need help. When you pray the words, "Thank you," let God know about some of the things he has done that make you smile and bring joy to your heart. Each day, let this prayer become a simple tool to express your heart to the One who loves you most and wants you to know that he is a trustworthy and good Father.

> The power of prayer depends on the One who hears the prayers, and the One who hears the prayer is my Daddy.

Living Lessons

God has placed people in your life who model prayer that is real, natural, and rooted in a confidence in their heavenly Father. These people are living prayer lessons for you to learn from. Identify two or three people who live the kind of prayer life you long to experience. Then, call one of these people and ask if he or she would be willing to help you learn about prayer during the weeks you are walking through the *Before Amen* group study. If the person is willing, try some (or all) of the following:

1. Interview the person about prayer. Keep notes that you can share with the rest of your group members. Here are some questions to get the conversation started:

   Who taught you to pray?

   How does prayer weave through the flow of your normal day?

   How does prayer connect you to God as your Father?

What advice would you give to someone who wants to grow deeper as a person of prayer?

Have you faced a time when it was hard to pray? If so, what helped you during that time?

Are there prayer pitfalls you could warn me to avoid?

2. Invite this person to pray *for* you during the coming four weeks as you learn to pray with greater passion, authenticity, and trust in your heavenly Father.

3. Ask the person if he or she would be willing to pray *with* you once a week during the four weeks of this small group learning experience. You could do this face-to-face or over the phone. As you pray with this person, seek to learn from his or her example and record any insights below.

Names Matter

In the coming four weeks, try to address God with new and fresh names. Each of God's names reflects an element of his character.

Begin by listing some names of God that you see used in Scripture and what the name expresses about him; a few examples have been provided. Use a Bible dictionary, concordance, or other reference tool, if necessary.

Then, as you pray, incorporate some of these names as the Spirit leads you.

Names:	Meaning (what it expresses):
Father	God provides for, protects, and loves me
Lord	He is in charge, the master, the ruler of my life
Savior	He died on the cross and rose again, paying the penalty for my sin

God has authority over the world ... and over *your* world.

Recommended Reading

As you reflect on what God is teaching you through this session, read chapters 1–3 of the book *Before Amen* by Max Lucado. In preparation for your next session, read chapters 4–6.

Journal, Reflections, and Notes

Session 2

I Need Help

Storms come crashing into our lives, our health teeters, our relationships fracture, our finances evaporate, and we can face the fragility of life and the uncertainty of almost everything we know. In these moments, Jesus extends this simple invitation: "Bring your problems to me." Here is the million-dollar question: Are we willing to utter these three words, "I need help," even if we have to choke them out?

Introduction

What is the first word a child learns and utters with confidence?

Dad delights when the first word is "papa" or "daddy." Mom beams with glee when it is "mama." Everyone thinks it is cute when the first word is "hi," "doggy," or "bye-bye." Sometimes, to a parent's dismay, that first word is "no"!

What about a first simple sentence? What does a little boy or girl learn to say early in life that can cause a parent to delight? Try this on for size: "I can do it all by myself!" There is a point when most children gain a sense of self-confidence and try to do things on their own. Sometimes they can actually deliver on their declaration, while at other times they can't quite accomplish it. Regardless, parents are proud that their baby is growing up and seeking independence. We want them to be self-sufficient. But this simple sentence that delights mothers and fathers can break the heart of our heavenly Father.

God delights when we say, "I need help!" Mature faith does not declare, "I can do it all by myself." Jesus died on the cross for our sins because we *can't* do it all by ourselves. The Holy Spirit came on the church and comes on every follower of Jesus because we *can't* do it all by ourselves. Our heavenly Father is ready to help, empower, uplift, guide, and save us when we recognize our need and call for help.

When you face hard times, what reflexive response do you say to your heavenly Father? "I can do it all by myself," or, "I need help"?

Jesus still asks, "What do you want me to do for you?"

Talk About It

What are some signs that we are relying on our own abilities when we face challenges in life?

or

What are some indicators that we recognize our need and are looking to God for help when we face tough times?

The moment you sense a problem, however large or small, take it to Christ.

Video Teaching Notes

As you watch the video teaching segment for Session 2 featuring Max Lucado, use the following outline to record anything that stands out to you.

Taking our problems to Jesus … the only One who can solve them

What happens when prayer meets real life

The story of the wedding in Cana of Galilee

In faith, we leave our problems with Jesus

The blind man crying out to Jesus over the crowd and the noise

Jesus still answers prayers for healing

Sickness of the soul: defensive and defeated

God specializes in guilt removal

> Guilt alerts us to the discrepancies between what we are and what God desires.

Video Discussion and Bible Study

1. Talk about a time when a "red engine light" came on in your life and the only option you had was to take this problem to Jesus.

> When the pieces of your life don't fit, take your problems to Jesus.

Read: Philippians 4:6–7

2. How can prayer help you overcome anxiety? How have you experienced the peace of God through an encounter with him in prayer?

3. Tell about an answered prayer that was specific, shocking, and faith-building.

4. What are you saying to God, yourself, and the world when you declare these words in prayer: "I need help"?

When you say, "I need help," you are telling God ...

When you say, "I need help," you are declaring to yourself ...

When you say, "I need help," you are witnessing to the world ...

Read: John 2:1–11

5. In the story of the wedding in Cana, Mary simply states the problem but is not emphatic about what Jesus should do about it. What does this teach us about how we pray and how much information we might need to give God?

What kind of patterns and habits mark your prayer life?

6. Max challenges us, "Take your problems to Jesus, not the bar, not out on others, not in temper tantrums, just to Jesus." Where do we tend to take our problems rather than bringing them to Jesus, trusting him, and then leaving them there?

Why is it hard to really leave our problems with Jesus and not keep carrying them in our heart, in our mind, or on our back?

> Resist the urge to reclaim the problem
> once you've given it up in prayer.

Read: Matthew 20:29–34

7. These blind men cried out for Jesus over the roar of the crowd, and they kept crying out even after people told them to be quiet. What are some ways that the world can try to silence us, stopping us from crying out to Jesus?

What can we do to keep crying out, even over the roar of the world and the voices that say, "Be quiet"?

8. God *will answer* all prayers for healing by followers of Jesus. Maybe this will happen immediately, maybe over time, and maybe when we see Jesus face-to-face, but healing is on the way. How can we embrace this truth and not become bitter if we don't get the healing in the timing or the way we might want?

> God will heal you: instantly or gradually or ultimately.

9. Max says this about defensive souls and defeated souls:

Defensive souls keep the skeleton in the closet. Tell no one. Admit nothing. Seek innocence, not forgiveness. Life is reduced to one aim: suppress the secret. Defeated souls are defined by the past. They didn't make a mistake; they are the mistake. They didn't foul up; they are a foul up. They don't hide the past; they wear it on their sleeve.

In what areas are you feeling defensive or defeated? How can your group members join you in prayer about this?

10. How would your life, attitudes, health, and relationships be different if you actually lived a truly guilt-free life?

What is *one* action you feel convicted to take in light of the truth shared in this session?

Open yourself to the idea of a guilt-free you.

Closing Prayer

Take time as a group to pray in any of the following directions:

- Confess how you seek to deal with challenges on your own when you should look to God for help, and then tell him you need his strength and presence.
- Thank God for a specific time that you cried out for his help and expressed your need, and he showed up and delivered you in a surprising and powerful way.
- Tell God what you are anxious about right now, and ask for his deep peace and trust to fill your heart.
- Pray for courage to come to Jesus, lay down your needs, and leave them with him … without trying to solve everything on your own.
- Intercede for one member of your group who dared to share an area of life that he or she is seeking to place before the loving heavenly Father.

God keeps his word. We just need to ask.

Between Sessions

Personal Reflection

Take time in personal reflection to think about the following questions:

- What are the situations in which my default button is to declare, "I can do it all by myself"? How can I begin calling out to God and saying, "I need your help"?
- Where do I have a defensive spirit right now? How can I surrender that spirit to my heavenly Father?
- What has caused me to feel defeated and beaten up? How can I place this challenge before God and trust him to heal me and help me through it?
- What is one need I seem to always try to meet the wrong way—a need that I have a hard time bringing to Jesus and leaving with him? What can I do to place this need in his able hands and not pick it up again?
- How has God shown up, healed, and delivered me when I have called out to him for help? How can remembering his faithfulness in the past give me confidence to trust him in the future?

Neither sin nor sickness will have dominion over God's people.

Personal Actions

Honest Evaluation ... Where I Need Help

Make a list of four areas in your life where you tend to trust yourself more than you should instead of calling upon God for his help:

Area 1: In Your _Relational_ Life

The area I tend to trust myself more than I should is ...

Some behaviors and patterns that show I am trusting myself ...

-
-
-

What I can do to place my trust in God and show him that I need his help ...

-
-
-

Specific ways I can pray, call out to God, and take action as led by his Spirit ...

-
-
-

Area 2: In Your _Spiritual_ Life

The area I tend to trust myself more than I should is ...

Some behaviors and patterns that show I am trusting myself ...

-
-
-

What I can do to place my trust in God and show him that I need his help ...

-
-
-

Specific ways I can pray, call out to God, and take action as led by his Spirit ...

-
-
-

Area 3: In Your _Financial and Economic_ Life

The area I tend to trust myself more than I should is ...

Some behaviors and patterns that show I am trusting myself . . .

-
-
-

What I can do to place my trust in God and show him that I need his help . . .

-
-
-

Specific ways I can pray, call out to God, and take action as led by his Spirit . . .

-
-
-

Area 4: In Your <u>Occupational</u> Life

The area I tend to trust myself more than I should is . . .

Some behaviors and patterns that show I am trusting myself . . .

-
-
-

What I can do to place my trust in God and show him that I need his help ...

-
-
-

Specific ways I can pray, call out to God, and take action as led by his Spirit ...

-
-
-

> God may use your struggle to change you.

Turning Down the Volume

The two blind men in Matthew 20 called out to Jesus over the noise of the crowd, and they pressed on even when people told them to back off. Sometimes we also need to press through resistance and overcome distractions and noise.

Set aside a twenty-minute block of time during the coming week during which you commit to shut off all technology, unplug all distractions, and get away from all the noise you can. Seek to come to God in silence. Then, ask him the specific questions that follow and wait quietly in his presence. If you feel promptings or identify the still, small voice of the Holy Spirit, write down the impressions you receive from God.

What are some of the areas of my life where I resist calling out for your help and tend to trust in my own abilities and strength?

How can I surrender these areas to you with greater consistency and humility?

Why am I afraid to place concerns and struggles in your hands and really trust you to handle them?

How have you proven yourself faithful and trustworthy in the past?

Instantly, Gradually, or Ultimately

God answers our prayers for healing—but never promised to answer them immediately or exactly as we expect. Make a list of four or five prayers for healing that you have lifted up to God in the past or are presently placing before him.

1.

2.

3.

4.

5.

After you have written down these prayers, indicate if God answered them quickly, after a time of trusting and patient waiting, or if you are still waiting for an answer.

Take a moment to thank God for the prayers that he answered "instantly." Celebrate that there are times when God sees, responds, and in his sovereign power decides to act immediately.

Look at the prayers that God answered after a time of waiting. For you this might have been a time of faith-filled trust or weeks and months of challenging patience. Praise God that he was with you throughout the process and acknowledge how he grew you spiritually as you walked on this journey of faith.

Reflect on the prayers that you are still placing in God's hands. Promise to leave them there. Continue to pray for these matters, but also trust that God knows and cares about them. Ask for patience in the waiting process and commit to God that you will love him, trust him, and follow him even if the final answer to your prayer comes on the other side of this life.

> If Jesus heals you instantly, praise him. If you are still waiting for healing, trust him. Your suffering is your sermon.

Recommended Reading

As you reflect on what God is teaching you through this session, read or reread chapters 4–6 of the book *Before Amen* by Max Lucado. In preparation for your next session, read chapter 7.

Journal, Reflections, and Notes

Session 3

They Need Help

When we know that God is a good Father and begin to ask him to meet our needs, something happens. He actually shows up and answers our prayers. Then another idea begins to grow in our mind and heart: What if God would hear my prayers for other people? What might happen if I prayed with confidence and faith for those I love and even for those who are difficult? What might God do?

Introduction

We have all faced those moments when we come to the end of our own abilities to help the ones we love and care about. It is a humbling reality.

Maybe our grown daughter is exhausted with the responsibility of raising three little ones, but there doesn't seem to be much we can do when we live three states away. Or, we want to help a buddy battle a powerful addiction, but we have no idea how to free our friend from the razor-sharp talons gripping his life. Or, we are walking with Dad through a long-term struggle with cancer and feel powerless to make things better. Or, our work colleague is fighting depression and we are frustrated that nothing we say or do seems to lift her spirits.

In these sobering moments, we realize we lack the power to heal broken hearts, infuse needed energy, restore ravaged bodies, lift emotional clouds, or multiply loaves of bread. In situations like these, we have to make a decision.

One option is to give up. When we acknowledge that our abilities are limited and our power to fix the lives of the people we love is not enough, we can quit. *What do I have to offer? I am in way over my head! This is too much for me to handle.* If we come to the end of our rope, we might find ourselves tempted to let go.

Jesus offers us a better option. In these moments — and they come to every one of us — we can look up and cry out to God for help. This is called intercession. It is all about asking God to help the people we love and the people who are tough to love. Once we have discovered that God is a good and loving Father, we not only ask him to help us, but we also dare to ask him to help other people ... because they need him too.

> Prayer works because God does.

Talk About It

Tell about a time when you came to the end of yourself and realized you simply did not have what another person needed. How did prayer factor into this situation? What difference did prayer make?

or

Tell about a time or season in your life when you really prayed for someone in your life with bold faith and a heart confident in God. What answers to prayer did you experience?

> We come to God in prayer with empty hands and high hopes.

Video Teaching Notes

As you watch the video teaching segment for Session 3 featuring Max Lucado, use the following outline to record anything that stands out to you.

When tragedy strikes ... what can you do?

A hot water bottle, a doll, and a lesson about prayer

Jesus' teaching about intercessory prayer in Luke 11:8–11

The difference between "belief" and "unbelief"

Moses' intercession for God's rebellious people

Our role as ambassadors for Christ

Intercessory prayer acknowledges our inability and God's ability

Pray for those you love and for those you do not

> Belief is pounding on God's door at
> midnight. Unbelief is attempting to help
> others without calling on Jesus.

Video Discussion and Bible Study

1. What keeps people from praying specific (hot water bottle
   and doll) prayers that are detailed and measurable? Why are
   these kinds of prayers important?

   Tell about a time when you or someone you know asked a
   specific and detailed prayer and then saw it answered.

Read: John 14:12 – 14

2. If we really believed everything Jesus says in this passage, how would it impact the way we pray? What stands in the way of us praying like this?

> When you knock on God's door, he responds quickly and fairly.

3. When times of loss, pain, and crisis hit the lives of the people you care about, how do you tend to respond? What are the first things that go through your mind and heart? What is the first thing you usually do?

Read: Luke 11:5 – 13

4. How does this parable paint a picture of bold and audacious prayer? What helps you to grow in boldness when it comes to asking God to help the people you love?

5. Jesus told some parables to draw a comparison and others to point out a contrast. This parable is meant to create a *contrast* between the reluctant neighbor and our willing and generous God. How is God's response to our prayers dramatically different than the neighbor's response to the late-night request?

6. After telling the story, Jesus assures us that God desires to answer our prayers (see Luke 11:9 – 10). He also uses two illustrations to show us that God is more generous than the best earthly parent (see Luke 11:11 – 13). On your own, take a couple of minutes to list five things you would ask God to do for people you care about if you really believed what Jesus says in this passage.

-

-

-

•

•

Tell your group about one or two of these prayers and invite them to join you in praying for God to help these people you care about.

> As we redouble our commitment to pray,
> God redoubles his promise to bless.

7. Who is one person who prayed for you to know Jesus long before you were born, or before you were interested in spiritual things, or before you were old enough to understand who Jesus was? How has God answered the prayers of this person?

Who is one person you are praying will come to understand the grace of God and open his or her heart to the love, forgiveness, and friendship of Jesus? How can your group members join you in asking God to move in the life of this person?

Read: Matthew 17:14–20

8. Jesus loved when people came to him with requests and supplications. He was willing to stop what he was doing to help them. What seemed to irritate Jesus was when people tried to take care of things themselves instead of bringing the need to him. What seems to be frustrating Jesus in this passage?

What are some situations in your life in which you are tempted to take care of things yourself—times when you should be running to Jesus and asking for his help? How can you develop a response pattern of going to Jesus first?

> Intercessory prayer acknowledges our
> inability and God's ability.

9. Max talks about how Moses prayed for the people of Israel after the whole "golden calf stunt" (see Exodus 32:1 – 14), and how God changed his mind and gave the nation another chance. Max makes two interesting statements:

   • *"God's ultimate will is inflexible, but the implementation of that will is not."*

   • *"We cannot change God's intention, but we can influence his actions."*

   Respond to these statements. Do you agree? Do you disagree? What are the implications for our prayer life if we agree with these statements?

10. What helps you pray more regularly, more confidently, and with greater boldness?

How will you engraft bold and faith-filled prayer into your life during the coming weeks? How can your group members support and encourage you in this pursuit?

Pray for all, before all, and above all.

Closing Prayer

Take time as a group to pray in any of the following directions:

- Thank God for specific and amazing answers to prayer that you (and the people you love) have received.
- Ask the Holy Spirit to give you faith and boldness to lift up specific, audacious prayers for others.
- Invite God to help you notice the needs around you with greater sensitivity so that you can engage in prayer for the people God has placed in your life.
- Confess those times you have trusted too much in your own ability to help others and have failed to knock on the door of heaven and make requests on behalf of others.
- Praise God for the high calling of being his ambassadors.

Praying for others is an awesome privilege and an awesome responsibility.

Between Sessions

Personal Reflection

Take time in personal reflection to think about the following questions.

- How has God proven himself faithful and trustworthy to answer prayer in my life? Why don't I pray more and with greater confidence?
- What is one specific, detailed, and important prayer that I have been reluctant to lift up to God? How can I begin knocking on his door about this concern?
- What are things I tend to do *before* I turn to prayer? How can I get to prayer quicker?
- Who is one person I tend to avoid praying for because he or she irritates me or doesn't treat me well? How could I begin praying for this person?

Personal Actions

A Huge and Meaningful Thank You

Identify a person who prays or prayed for you faithfully for months or years. If this person has passed away and is with Jesus, think of a way you could honor that individual by sharing his or her story with others. If the person is alive, think of some ways you can honor and thank that individual for the amazing impact he or she has had on your life. It could be a dinner or a party in his or her honor. You might write a poem, a short story, or a testimony to share with that person and others. You could record a short video telling about all the ways God used that person to impact your life, and then send it to him or her and post it on a social media site. Be creative!

Person: _____

Action I can take:

Noticing Needs and Knocking on Heaven's Door

Identify three places God has put you where you can be a powerful presence of supplication and intercessory prayer. During the next couple of weeks, make a point of noticing specific people and gathering needs for prayer.

Step One: Identify the Places

First, identify the places you will be noticing people and needs. This could be your home, school, workplace, neighborhood, church, a social gathering, a place you volunteer, where you shop, or anywhere you find yourself on a regular basis.

Place 1

Place 2

Place 3

Step Two: Identify the People

Next, identify one to three people in each place who you want to begin praying for and lifting up before the Lord. Note them on the left side below.

People in place 1:   *Specific needs I will pray for:*

-
-
-

People in place 2:   *Specific needs I will pray for:*

-
-
-

People in place 3:   *Specific needs I will pray for:*

-
-
-

Step Three: Identify the Prayers

Write down one to two specific prayers you will lift up for each person on your list, using the space provided on the previous page. If watching and noticing does not give you a sense of how to pray, ask the people themselves what you might pray for. Most people are glad to have someone pray for them, even if they are not people of faith.

Step Four: Knock on Heaven's Door

Now you will want to knock on the door of heaven for each of these people and their needs. Do this once each day for seven to ten days. Pray in faith, be specific, and place these needs in the hands of the God who loves these people more than you do.

Step Five: List Answered Prayers

Make a list of prayers you have seen God answer during the days you have been knocking on his door for these people.

Step Six: Contact the People

Finally, let these people know that you have been praying for them, and then give God the praise for answering your requests in specific and powerful ways.

If you find this experience to be powerful for you and for others, return to step one and choose some new people for whom you will intercede—and continue with the people you have already been praying for!

> You are never more like Jesus than when
> you pray for others.

Reminders and Testimonies

Get an object that reminds you of a powerful and specific answer to prayer in your life or the life of someone else. (Some examples might include a baptism picture of a family member you prayed would come to faith in Christ, an ultrasound image showing a baby in the womb of someone you prayed would be able to conceive, or a souvenir from a country where a family member or friend returned home safely after you prayed for him or her.) Place this object on a shelf in your home, on your desk at work, on the dashboard of your car, or in some other place where you (and others) will see it.

Each time you see this object, remember how God answers prayer with clarity and power. If someone asks about the object, share the story behind it and how God showed up and answered your prayer in an amazing way. This testimony will not only inspire other followers of Jesus but may cause non-believers to wonder if God is real and could answer *their* prayers. Hopefully, it will inspire you to keep growing in your prayer journey.

If you can't think of an object from an answered prayer in your life, just put a hot water bottle and a doll someplace where you and others will see them. If anyone asks about them, share how they are a reminder of the power of prayer, and then tell the story of Dr. Roseveare and a little orphan in the Congo.

> Jesus never refused an intercessory request. Ever!

Recommended Reading

As you reflect on what God is teaching you through this session, read or reread chapter 7 of the book *Before Amen* by Max Lucado. In preparation for your next session, read chapters 8 and 9.

Journal, Reflections, and Notes

Session 4

Thank You

Thanksgiving is the gateway to life, joy, obedience, perspective, hope, victory, friendship with God, and more than we dream. Ingratitude is the fast track leading to sin, rebellion, suspicion, loneliness, selfishness, and death. Choose life, open your eyes to God's goodness, and say, "Thank you!"

Introduction

We have all heard it said that there are two kinds of people in the world: those who see the cup half full and those who see the cup half empty.

The truth is that there is another group of people who don't get mentioned in this equation. These folks see the world in a third way — a beautiful way; a faith-filled way; a thankful way. These are the people who see the cup entirely full and overflowing!

When we look at the world with eyes fixed on Jesus, live with unyielding gratitude, notice God's good gifts, and say "thank you" with a sincere heart, our cup can always be full. There could be a water shortage, or we could be in a desert, or someone could be doing his or her best to turn off the faucet, but the presence of Jesus and a grateful spirit are always enough to fill our cup and leave us with plenty of refreshing water to spare.

If you tend to be a cup-half-empty person, ask Jesus to help you notice and appreciate the countless blessings and infinite good gifts he has poured into your life. If you are a cup-half-full person, make a decision today that you will never again be content with half a cup. Ask God to open your eyes to see the roaring, raging river of goodness available to you, and then pray for your heart to be filled to overflowing.

One of these days, someone will be talking to you and the old cup-half-full or cup-half-empty discussion will come up. Refuse these limited options. Look the person in the eye, smile, and say, "I see the cup entirely full! As a matter of fact, my cup runs over."

To say "thanks" is to celebrate a gift.

Talk About It

How might our outlook on life change if we saw the cup full and overflowing rather than half full or half empty?

or

How can a grateful heart and a commitment to express thankfulness for the little and big gifts of God fill our cup to overflowing?

To say thanks to God causes us to recognize that regardless of our circumstances, we are truly blessed.

Video Teaching Notes

As you watch the video teaching segment for Session 4 featuring Max Lucado, use the following outline to record anything that stands out to you.

We can find beauty and hope during the hard seasons of life

The power and impact of a thankful spirit, even in the face of suffering

Thankfulness is a command, not a suggestion or recommendation

How to make a perfect place imperfect ... ingratitude

Lessons from God's people in the desert

We should be thankful for what God gives and recognize his great gifts

The undeniable and unimpeachable authority of Jesus

Praying in the name of Jesus is not an empty motto or talisman

> God's solution to any challenge is to have a grateful spirit.

Video Discussion and Bible Study

1. Tell about someone you have watched and studied over the years who seemed to always have a spirit of thankfulness for the goodness of God, no matter what he or she was facing.

2. When is it most difficult for you to say thank you to the people in your life? When is it toughest to stop and say thank you to God?

3. In this session, Max shares his story about how he is dealing with pain in his writing hand. Although he has prayed about it, God has not yet removed the pain. Max says, "I want God to heal my hand. So far, he has used my hand to heal my heart." What do you think Max is getting at with this statement? How is this an answer to his prayers?

How can Max's attitude encourage us in some of the struggles of our own lives?

No mist is so thick that the sunlight of appreciation can't burn it away.

Read: 1 Thessalonians 5:18

4. We are called to give thanks in *all* circumstances. Why do you think God is so emphatic and concerned that we learn to live thankfully?

What is a circumstance you are facing right now that makes it difficult to be thankful? How can your group members support you in prayer and encourage you as you seek to walk through this circumstance with a thankful spirit?

"In all circumstances" means when we are *in* trouble, *in* the hospital, *in* a fix, *in* a mess, *in* discomfort, or *in* distress. It means to follow the example of Jesus, who was robustly thankful on all occasions.

Read: Genesis 3:1 – 13

5. What did the serpent do that created discontent and ingratitude in the hearts of Adam and Eve?

What were some of the results and consequences of Adam and Eve's journey into ingratitude?

6. Satan enticed Adam and Eve to look away from all of the good things they had and to fixate instead on what they did not have. He uses this same tactic today. What are some ways Satan uses our culture, the media, the people around us, or the hidden desires of our hearts to create discontent and drive us to spend our time and energy pursuing what we don't yet have?

What are some practical ways we can battle these entice-ments, plug our ears, block our eyes, and resist being sucked into a life of always wanting what we don't have?

Ingratitude is the original sin.

Read: Exodus 16:3 – 7, 13 – 16, 31 – 32 and Numbers 11:4 – 6

7. As you read these passages, what do you learn about God and about his people? In what ways are our attitudes and actions often similar to those of the Israelites in this account?

Read: Numbers 21:4–9

8. As severe as the picture painted in this passage might be, read it closely and let the lesson wash over you. How seriously does God take ingratitude?

By God's grace, we live on the other side of the cross. Even as the people of Israel could look up and see the bronze snake and be healed, so we can look up and see Jesus crucified for our sins and be saved. Tell about when you became a follower of Jesus and how looking to him helps you live a grateful and thankful life.

Read: Matthew 8:5–10

9. What did the centurion in this story understand about authority in general and Jesus' authority in particular?

How is confident prayer a declaration that we understand and believe in the power and authority of Jesus?

> We have access to the throne room of
> God by virtue of the name of Jesus.

10. What are some practical ways we can express thankfulness and a grateful heart during *any* of these moments we face in a normal day:

    ❑ When we first wake up
    ❑ When we stand in front of the mirror and prepare ourselves for the day
    ❑ When we stand looking into an open clothes closet
    ❑ When we encounter a person who is difficult and prickly
    ❑ When we bump into a person who is gracious and kind
    ❑ When we hear good news
    ❑ When we receive bad news
    ❑ When we sit at a meal
    ❑ When we get stuck in traffic, in an elevator, or in a tough conversation
    ❑ When we put our head on the pillow at the end of the day

How do we die with gratitude? Simple.
We live with it.

Closing Prayer

Take time as a group to pray in any of the following directions:

- Thank God for the people in your life who model a heart of gratitude.
- Thank God for people who stretch you, challenge you, and drive you to your knees in prayer.
- Thank God for his Word—the Bible—and how it instructs, encourages, and directs you each day.
- Thank Jesus for being the absolute authority in the universe and that you can trust him at all times.
- Ask for strength to be thankful, even when times are hard and pain is close at hand.

Prayer changes things because prayer
appeals to the top power in the universe.

In the Coming Days

Personal Reflection

Take time in personal reflection to think about the following questions:

- When is it hardest for me to be thankful? What are the times when I am tempted to see the cup of my life as half empty? How can I focus on Jesus in these times and remain grateful?
- Satan seeks to get my eyes off God's good gifts so I can be consumed with desire for the things I don't have. How is the enemy using this tactic in my life? What can I do to battle against his distractions and enticements?
- Am I truly confident in the absolute and infinite authority of Jesus? If so, how can I walk in greater confidence as his child? If not, how will I ask Jesus to help me grow my confidence in his authority?

Prayer is the "Yes" to God's invitation to invoke his name.

Personal Actions

Keeping Our Eyes on the Right Things

Satan convinced Adam and Eve to look away from all the good things they had and to fixate on what was off limits. It is the oldest trick in the book ... literally! The enemy of our souls is working out of the same playbook he used in Eden because it still works ... most of the time. However, we can battle his enticements by making a choice to focus our attention, our eyes, our hearts, and our desires on the good things God has already given us.

List two or three good gifts God has given you in each of the following areas:

In your *family life* ...

-
-
-

In your *professional life* ...

-
-
-

In your *spiritual life* ...

-
-
-

In your *relational life* ...

-
-
-

In your *recreational life* ...

-
-
-

In *some other area* of your *life* (your choice!) ...

-
-
-

When you find your eyes, your heart, your mind, or your desires wandering, read this list. Read it slowly, read it aloud, and even add a few new items. Remind yourself of how good God has been and focus on his amazing grace and many gifts. Don't fall for Satan's old tricks!

Share the Prayer

If God has used this simple prayer to impact your life, teach it to someone else:

> *Father,*
> *You are good.*
> *I need help.*
> *They need help.*
> *Thank you.*
> *In Jesus' name, amen.*

You might want to teach this prayer to a child, a grandchild, a parent, or a sibling. Maybe you can pass it on to a neighbor, a coworker, or a friend. You could share it with your pastor, a church board member, or a Sunday school teacher. You might want to give someone a copy of the *Before Amen* book or just write out the prayer, give it to the person, and tell him or her how it has impacted your life. If God has grown your faith in him and your relationship with Jesus through this small group study, share the prayer!

> On the occasions you can't find the words to say, pull these out of your pocket: "Father, you are good. I need help. They need help. Thank you. In Jesus' name, amen."

A-Z Prayer

In *Before Amen*, Max lists things and people he is thankful for from A to Z. Take some time in the coming week to make your own list of things God has given, provided, or allowed you to experience. Try to list two or three things that start with each letter. Have fun with it. Then, when you have made your list, read it slowly, prayerfully—and thankfully!

A—   D—

B—   E—

C—   F—

G—   Q—

H—   R—

I—   S—

J—   T—

K—   U—

L—   V—

M—   W—

N—   X—

O—   Y—

P—   Z—

Prayer is good because God is good.

Recommended Reading

As you reflect on what God is teaching you through this session, read or reread chapters 8 and 9 of the book *Before Amen* by Max Lucado.

Journal, Reflections, and Notes

Small Group Leader Helps

To ensure a successful small group experience, read the following information before beginning.

Group Preparation

Whether your small group has been meeting together for years or is gathering for the first time, be sure to designate a consistent time and place to work through the four sessions. Once you establish the when and where of your times together, select a facilitator who will keep discussions on track and an eye on the clock. If you choose to rotate this responsibility, assign the four sessions to their respective facilitators up front so that group members can prepare their thoughts and questions prior to the session they are responsible for leading. Follow the same assignment procedure should your group want to serve any snacks/beverages.

A Note to Facilitators

As facilitator, you are responsible for honoring the agreed-upon time frame of each meeting, for prompting helpful discussion among your group, and for keeping the dialogue equitable by drawing out quieter members and helping more talkative members to remember that others' insights are valued in your group.

You might find it helpful to preview each session's video teaching segment (they range from 16–21 minutes) and then scan the discussion questions and Bible passages that pertain to it, highlighting various questions that you want to be sure to cover during your group's meeting. Ask God in advance of your time together to guide your group's discussion, and then be sensitive to the direction he wishes to lead.

Urge participants to bring their study guide, pen, and a Bible to every gathering. Encourage them to consider buying a copy of the book *Before Amen* by Max Lucado to supplement this study.

Session Format

Each session of the study guide includes the following group components:

- **"Introduction"**—an entrée to the session's topic, which may be read by a volunteer or summarized by the facilitator
- **"Talk About It"**—icebreaker questions that relate to the session topic and invite input from every group member (select one, or use both options if time permits)

- **"Video Teaching Notes"**—an outline of the session's video teaching segment for group members to follow along and take notes if they wish
- **"Video Discussion and Bible Study"**—video-related and Bible exploration questions that reinforce the session content and elicit personal input from every group member
- **"Closing Prayer"**—several prayer cues to guide group members in closing prayer

Additionally, in each session you will find a **"Between Sessions"** section (**"In the Coming Days"** for Session 4) that includes a personal reflection, suggestions for personal actions, recommended reading from the *Before Amen* book, and a journaling opportunity.

Discover Even More Power in a Simple Prayer

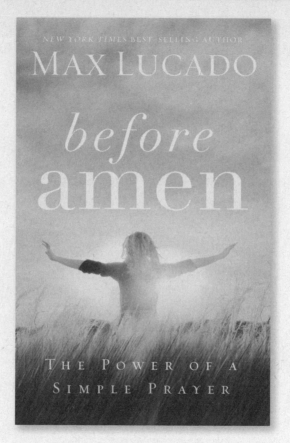

ISBN 978-0-8499-4848-0

$19.99

Join Max Lucado on a journey to the very heart of biblical prayer and discover rest in the midst of chaos and confidence even for prayer wimps.

Available wherever books are sold.

BeforeAmen.com

Make Your Prayers Personal

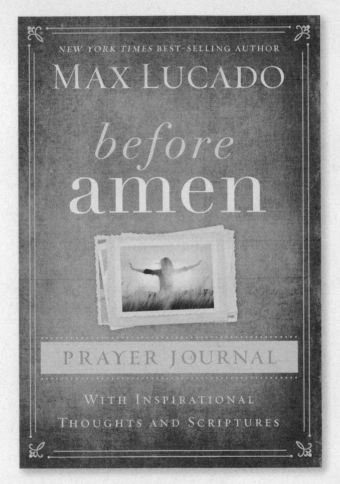

ISBN 978-0-7180-1406-3

$13.99

This beautiful companion journal to *Before Amen* helps readers stoke their prayer life. It features quotes and scriptures to inspire both prayer warriors and those who struggle to pray.

More Tools for Your Church and Small Group

Before Amen Church Campaign Kit

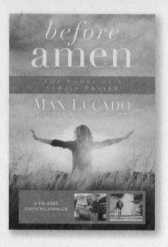

ISBN 978-0-529-12369-5
$49.99

The church campaign kit includes a four-session DVD study by Max Lucado; a study guide with discussion questions and video notes; the *Before Amen* trade book; a getting started guide; and access to a website with all the sermon resources churches need to launch and sustain a four-week *Before Amen* campaign.

Pocket Prayers: 40 Simple Prayers that Bring Peace and Rest

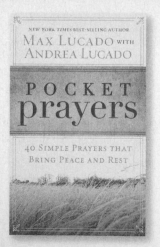

ISBN 978-0-7180-1404-9
$2.99

Includes forty pocket-sized prayers written specifically for times of uncertainty and turmoil. It's ideal for churches and ministries to use as an outreach tool.